The Great Secret Of The Flower Of Life And The Light Liquid Of The Gods.
The Mushroom Symbol, The Knights Templar and Early Christianity

Dirasat 139 given in 1964, in Cairo, Egypt.

*** *** ***

Copyright ©2015 by Maximillien de Lafayette. All rights reserved. No part of this book may be used or reproduced by any means, graphic, electronic, or mechanical, including photocopying, recording, taping or by any information storage retrieval system without the written permission of the author except in the case of brief quotations embodied in critical articles and reviews.

Published by Times Square Press, New York, Berlin.
Date of Publication: August 20, 2015

Recent Books by Maximillien de Lafayette

1-Your astral body and your parallel double, lecture 115,
2-2015 best psychics, mediums and lightworkers in the United States
3-2015 Europe's best psychics and mediums: Meilleurs Médiums et Voyants en France et Europe (Most effective and honest lightworkers in Europe)
4-National & International Rank of the World's Best Lightworkers (The Best Psychics and Mediums in the World)
5-Encyclopedic dictionary of djinn, sihr and spiritism languages. Vocabulary, Phraseology and Dictionary Of The Languages Of Sahiriin, Djinn, Afarit, Shayatiin, Spirits, Witchcraft.
6-How to Talk to Spirits, Ghosts, Entities, Angels and Demons: Techniques & Instructions: The Most Powerful Commands and Spells
7-Instructions and Techniques for Commanding Spirits and Communicating with Angels and Entities. 7th Edition
8-5th Edition. Your Lucky Hours and Unlucky Hours in Your Life from Monday To Sunday. How to bring good luck to your life.
9-The origin of the name of god and his true identity. Synopsis and translation of the Phoenician, Ugaritic, Canaanite, Sumerian, Akkadian, and Assyrian tablets.
10-The Supersymetric mind: Activation of the conduit and the Supersymetric mind; beyond the third eye and toward the oneness.
11-How to Use Your Mind Power to do the Impossible: Esoteric techniques to activate the mental power of your mind.
12-When Heaven Calls You: Connection with the Afterlife, Spirits, 4th Dimension, 5th Dimension, Higher-Self, Astral Body, Parallel Dimensions and the Future.
13-The essential Maximillien de Lafayette. The official Anunnaki Ulema textbook for the teacher and the student. (The road to enlightenment and ultimate knowledge)

En route:
1-Foreseeing passages from you future and rewinding time.
2-The whole truth about the afterlife.
3-A mother calling her son from beyond the grave.
4-Please don't die without me.
5-Everything you need to know about Djinn.

*** *** ***

ACKNOWLEDGMENT AND GRATITUDE

I am deeply grateful to the Honorable Ulema, Anunnaki-Ulema, Cheiks, Allamah, Gurus, and Asaatiza, who have guided me in this work:

Anunnaki-Ulema, The Right Honorable Cheik Al Baydani
Anunnaki-Ulema Mordachai ben Zvi
Anunnaki-Ulema Ayira Kermaat
Allamah Subhi Al Barazani
Grand Master, Ulema Dr. Farid Tayarah
Shaman Shabalah Erirou Ataneh
Allamah Kader Al Tabrizi
Allamah Shaker El Diin
Allamah Suleiman Sharaf El Diin
Allamah Cheik Talal Salem Al Badri
Allamah Cheik Khalid Al Faqueeh
Cheik Suleiman Al Habashi
Cheik Waleed Subhi Al Yamani
Allamah Cheik Ala' Alaweh Ayeelou

For without their help and guidance, this book would have remained the shadow of an idea in my drawers.

*** *** ***

Maximillien de Lafayette

THE GREAT SECRET OF THE FLOWER OF LIFE AND THE LIGHT LIQUID OF THE GODS.
The Mushroom Symbol, The Knights Templars and Early Christianity.

The Great Secret Of The Flower Of Life And The Light Liquid Of The Gods.
The Mushroom Symbol, The Knights Templar and Early Christianity

Maximillien de Lafayette

Transcribed by
Marla Cohen
Liza Coleman

Times Square Press
New York   Berlin
2015

Table Of Contents

- Filfila "Fil-I-fila": Name for an esoteric symbol closely related to the Anunnaki's "Light Liquid" and the "Flower of Life".
- Perhaps the following excerpt from the Anunnaki-Ulema Kira'at, could elucidate the matter.
- The mushroom symbol and Knights Templar.
- The mushroom symbol and Christianity.
- Arwad.
- Hafnah-Baricha.
- Definition and introduction.
- Creative energy
- Anunnaki-Ulemite mushroom and the "Sacred Halo" and Holy Grail.
- Hafnah-Baricha: The extract of mushroom blended with a non-human DNA,
- I. Definition and introduction.
- II. Creative energy.
- III. Anunnaki-Ulemite mushroom and the "Sacred Halo" and Holy Grail.
- Nicolas Flamel and the "Light Liquid".

*** *** ***

FILFILA "FIL-I-FILA"

ANUNNAKI'S "LIGHT LIQUID" AND THE "FLOWER OF LIFE".

Filfila "Fil-I-fila"
Ana'kh/Ulemite. Noun.

Name for an esoteric symbol closely related to the Anunnaki's "Light Liquid" and the "Flower of Life".
Literally it means a rose.
And the rose represents a magical chalice.
Some time, the chalice itself.
Quite often, this chalice was depicted as a mushroom.
It is quite obvious, that the chalice, the rose, the Flower of Life are symbols.

In the black arts, esoterism, so-called magic, and other secret esoteric and occult teachings and principles, behind each symbol, there is another secret symbol, and behind each depiction or illustration, there is another secret illustration and depiction.
Filfila is no exception.

***   ***   ***

Perhaps the following excerpt from the Anunnaki-Ulema Kira'at, could elucidate the matter:
"…The meaning of the name of the great Perseus, founder of the Perseid Dynasty, and builder of the citadel of Mycenae is: "The Place of the Mushroom", and various illustrations of the mushroom appear abundantly on churches' columns.

Another striking example is the figure of the Biblical Melchizedek that appeared on a façade of the Cathedral de Chartre in France, holding a chalice in the shape of a mushroom, symbolizing life, and perhaps the Holy Grail, as interpreted in the literature of Cathars, Knights Templar, and many enlightened eastern secret societies.

It was also interpreted as the "Divine-Human Vessel", meaning the womb of Virgin Mary; the very womb that gave birth to Jesus.

In ancient Phoenician and Akkadian traditions closely related to the Anunnaki, the mushroom as a chalice represents the creative power of the female.
More precisely, the fecundity of a female Anunnaki goddess, giver of life and all living creatures.
This fecundity source came in the form of a mitochondrial DNA. Also, the secret extracted liquid of the mushroom represented the "Light Liquid" known also as Elixir of Life.

*** *** ***

The mushroom symbol and Knights Templar.
On many Templars' pillars and Bourj (Upper part of a medieval fortress or a castle) in Syria, Malta and Lebanon, the mushroom is carefully illustrated as a "Flower of Life" known to the Phoenicians, Habiru (Hebrew), early Arabs, Sumerians and Anunnaki as:

- **a**-Wardah
- **b**-Ward
- **c**-Vardeh

These three words (Meaning a rose, or a flower) in ancient linguistic context, symbolized the blooming of life.
At one point in history, the mushroom's figure was used by the Templar Order of St. John of Malta as the symbol of the Holy Grail.
And in other passages, the mushroom represented a head; the head of a Sinhar "A leader".

Some historians thought that the leader was Baphomet, while others believed it was Noah, and another group believed it was the Prophet Mohammed, and finally, there is a group of learned masters who claimed that is was the Khalek of Markabah.

Khalek is one of the seventy two names/attributes of God in Arabic (Now, 99), and Markabah or Merkabah means a spaceship in Sumerian and Akkadian.

***   ***   ***

Mass burning of the Cathars.
They paid a high price because of their esoteric beliefs.

Montségur, in Southern France, the last stronghold of the Cathars.

Pre-Columbian "Guatemala" mushroom-priest, who was in charge of esoteric-magical ritual ceremonies, similar to the Phoenician Melkart's ceremonies in Arwad, and Amrit.

Baal of Arwad.

The worship ceremony of the Phoenician-Ugaritic god Baal included Maharit rituals (Elixir of life). According to "Ilmu Al Donia", it was this very Maharit which gave legendary longevity to ancient Biblical patriarchs and Anunnaki-Mesopotamian rulers.

The Phoenician Temple of Melkart at Amrit.

Around this ancient Phoenician monument, the ritual ceremony of Mahrit took place.

Melkart of Carthage.

The Melkart's Shrines at Carthage (Modern Tunis) and Amrit were decorated with Anunnaki motifs and symbols, such as the Arwad Serpent representing wisdom, knowledge and science, and the Tyrian moon crescent, representing new birth, and the Anunnaki Delta-Tyrian Triangle, representing the equilibrium of nature and man.

Ruins of the Phoenician cemetery of Amrit. The reverse crescent on the central slab of the cemetery represent Mahrit (Maharit) and "Light Liquid".

Arwad

Phoenician tombs on the Island of Arwad (Syria).

The Island of Arwad was an independent kingdom in the days of the Canaanites. It was created by the Phoenicians in early second millennium B.C. This small beautiful island located 5 miles from the city of Tartus in Syria, was one of the first Anunnaki's small colonies on earth.

It was mentioned in the Bible by the Prophet Ezekiel. Arwad was the headquarters of the seven wise men who came from Apsu, the sweet water, and attended God Enki.

They were known to the Sumerians as Abgal, to the Akkadians as Akkallu, and to the Phoenicians as An-Khal. The Anunnaki called them "The Ab-n'GAL."

On the Island of Arwad, the Phoenicians created a secret society called the "Circle of the Serpent" to honor their god Melkart. The Melkart shrine/altar still stands in all its beauty and majestic architecture. It was during the ceremony of the worship of Melkart, that the Maharit was elevated to the status of "Ligh Liquid", the elixir of life of the immortal gods.

The early learned Greeks who visited Arwad studied medicine at the Phoenician-Anunnaki medical center, and when they returned home, they adopted the Phoenician sign of the serpent as the logo for their healing arts.

Island of Arwad, where Phoenicians created a secret society called the "Circle of the Serpent" to honor god Melkart. Arwad is mentioned in the Bible by the Prophet Ezekiel.

Harbor of Arwad.

The Castle of Arwad.

St. John Chapel in Byblos.

In 1939, the Vichy Government found in the basement of St. John Chapel, an Ana'kh manuscript detailing the early blueprints of the chapel retracing the history and a meticulous description of a Phoenician temple which served as an esoteric center for Maharit and "Light Liquid" used by the early remnants of the Anunnaki.
In addition to the blueprints, a tablet was discovered under the second layer of the chapel's foundation, containing an archaic illustration of the Ana'kh symbols.

*** *** ***

This painting depicts the coronation ceremony of the first Christian Emperor, Constantine The great. The umbrella-shape right above Constantine's head is an esoteric mushroom representation.

The Fountain in St. Peter's Square in the Vatican, is a perfect example of the esoteric representation of the mushroom.

The Anunnaki's mushroom symbol gave birth to the "Cult of Head". Anne Ross in her book "Pagan Celtic Britain", wrote: "The Cult of the Human Head constitutes a persistent theme throughout all aspects of Celtic life spiritual and temporal and the symbol of the severed head may be regarded as the most typical and universal of their religious attitudes."

*** *** ***

The mushroom symbol and Christianity.
The Anunnaki's mushroom also influenced early Christian royal coronation ceremonies, such as the coronation of the first Christian Emperor, Constantine The Great.
It also shaped several early hidden Christian symbols, including Catholic architecture in the eastern and western hemispheres, particularly, the Fountain in St. Peter's Square in the Vatican.

*** *** ***

HAFNAH-BARICHA

CREATIVE ENERGY.

Hafnah-Baricha
Ana'kh/Ulemite. Noun.

I. Definition and introduction.
II. Creative energy.
III. Anunnaki-Ulemite mushroom and the "Sacred Halo" and Holy Grail.

I. Definition and introduction:
Derived from the Ana'kh-Ulemite word "Hafnah".
In my previous books, I have discussed the concept of Hafnah at length, and explained its relation to the primordial source of energy of life-forms, including human life.
So, I will not repeat the same information in this book.

The word "Hafnah-Baricha" means the extract of mushroom blended with a non-human DNA, the ancients in the Near East and the Middle East used to prolong life, and in some instances, to create life itself.
This knowledge was transformed into a cult, known as the Hafnahbarickha, meaning the cult of the mushroom.

Arwadians and early Phoenicians and Ugarit's priests developed the cult into an elaborate secret ritual.
Later on, neighboring civilizations have adopted the ritual, and transformed it into a worship ritual, without discovering its secret esoteric meaning, and the implications of the use of the "Hafnah-Baricha".

*** *** ***

II. Creative energy.

Anunnaki Ulema Ghandar and Ben Zvi have explained that the world, including all life-forms were created by a "Feminine Energy".
In other words, some sort of a "Female Power".
This creative energy was represented by a mushroom.
The very same mushroom that has appeared in religious ornaments and statues, decorating the façade of many Gothic churches in Europe.

The mushroom is one of the primordial symbols and signs used by the Anunnaki in Phoenicia and Mesopotamia.
In some of the Babylonian cylinders, the mushroom is depicted as a rosette. In fact, the Akkadian-Sumerian tablets, as well as Anunnaki's inscriptions in the Book of Ramadosh, and "Ilmu Donia" (Science of the World or Universe) referred to goddesses and female energy that have shaped the known cosmos, and gave a life-form to everything that has existed on Earth.
Early Gnostics and mystics in Anatolia have claimed that the early Gnostic form of Christianity has accepted this concept.

In fact, many of the early Gnostic Church doctors wore a toga decorated with mushroom flowers.
Madame Helena Petrovna Blavatsky has said, "The pallium, or ancient stole of the bishop, is the feminine sign when worn by a priest in worship."

*** *** ***

III. Anunnaki-Ulemite mushroom and the "Sacred Halo" and Holy Grail.

According to Ulema Master Li, even the Jewish Yamulka and the canopy used in early Christian coronation ceremonies are a vivid but secret symbol of the Anunnaki's mushroom.

The Hindu, Buddhists and early Christians transformed the shape of a mushroom into a "Sacred Halo", as sign of enlightenment and sainthood.

The Anunnaki Sinhars were always depicted as super-beings with a halo over their heads.

Anunnaki-Ulema Al Bakri stated in one of his Kira'at, that the Knights Templar depicted the Holy Grail as a divine symbol of the "Holy mushroom Amanita Muscaria", and vice versa.

In the ritual ceremony of the "Serpent Circle" of Milkart on the Island of Arwad, the "Holy Mushroom" was always visible on Milkart's altar, as a sign of health, life, and healing power.

*** *** ***

Nicolas Flamel and the "Light Liquid".

Two legendary figures of the occult worked with the "Light Liquid" and a secret "extraction" from a rare species of mushrooms found in the Middle East: Saint Germain, and Nicola Flamel.

Madame Blavatsky with Kuthumi, El Myora, and Anunnaki-Ulema Saint Germain. Image supposedly taken in the late 1800's.

Nicolas Flamel (1330-1418?) was a famous alchemist and an Anunnaki Ulema. It is thought that he was born in Pontoise, but spent most of his life in Paris, where he started his business in a stall for selling his manuscripts.

Home of Nicolas Flamel, transformed into an auberge (Inn).

His business prospered, and eventually he bought a house and used the in Rue de Marivaux, using the ground floor for his business.

Nicolas Flamel

Nicolas Flamel hired other scriveners, copyists, and illuminators, and gave writing lessons to the members of the noble families who wished to learn.
Years after his death, his totally unknown expose on "Beings of Lights" (Anunnaki) was discovered in Marseille, France. In his essay, Flamel wrote about the celestial gods (Gods) who created the "First Man" and the alchemy work "Light Liquid" carried by the Phoenicians in ancient Phoenicia and Syria.

Flamel was a great alchemist and a believer in the return of the Anunnaki, however, he was more known as "The Master of Minerals" than an Anunnaki Ulema.
It was not so much the transmutation of metals into gold that interested him, even though that would be good too, but the idea of discovering the secrets of nature, of immortality, of wisdom, that appealed to him.

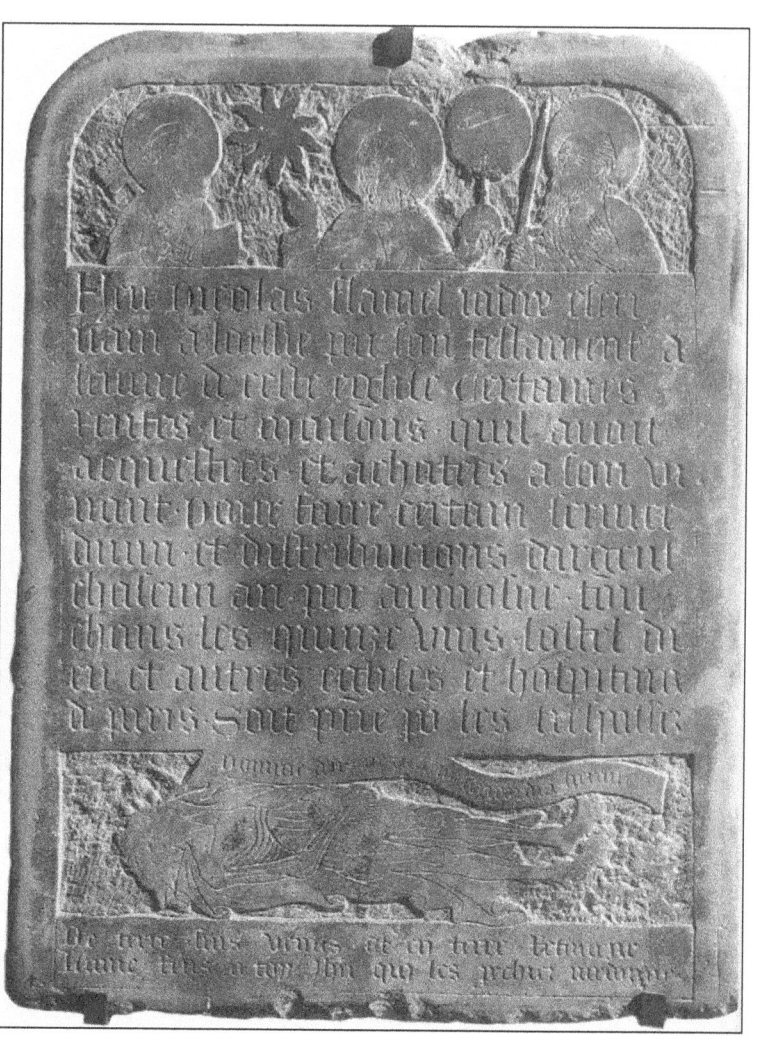

Flamel's tomb stone.

He heard that the secrets were written down in a book, somewhere, and he kept his eyes open to any mysterious manuscript that came his way.

And one day a poor man who obviously needed money sold him a slender little book, bound with an old copper cover with some interesting engraving. The leaves were made of old parchment, on which the writing was clearly done.

It had only twenty-one pages, divided into three part, each separated by a blank page, all edged with gold. He could only understand some of the words, but many were written in a language he had never seen. The first page was clear – the book was written by one Abraham the Jew, who was a prince of his people, a Levite (priest, or servant at the Temple), astrologer, and philosopher.

*** *** ***

Just Published!
Don't miss these extraordinary books by Maximillien de Lafayette

---

Calendar of Hours & Days Which Bring You Bad Luck & Good Luck: How to Positively Change your Future

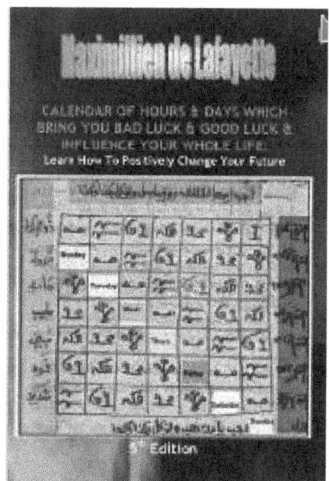

What is luck?
Merriam-Webster's definition of "Luck":
a- A force that brings good fortune or adversity.
b- The events or circumstances that operate for or against an individual.
But what is that "force" that brings good fortune or adversity? And how events or circumstances "operate" for or against an individual?
Merriam-Webster does not provide an explanation.
There is a force that shapes and conditions luck; it is the force of the Maktoob, meaning what it is already written in the "Kitbu Dounia", meaning the book of our life, the book of our fate; the book of our destiny.
And how do we explain the mode of operation of events or circumstances that work for us or against us?

47

The mode of operation of what constitutes "Luck" is always conditioned by unseen metaphysical factors, only known to the Anunnaki Ulema and Sahiriin.
Basically, these factors include:
Factors which influence your future and luck:
• Maktoob.
The fluctuation of the "Grid of Calendar" of the good hours and bad hours in our lives: Rizmanah. The calendar of hours and days of your life which bring you good luck and bad luck.

• Some hours are positive, others negative.
Kharta-Makan, which means your zone. In other words, where you live; the location of your home, office, and other places you have lived at and/or you shall occupy in the future.
Ismu, which means your name. It is very true that your name plays a paramount role on the landscape of your luck, future, success and failures.
In summary, time, places and even your name are part of the scenario of the film of your life on the screen of your existence on Earth, and beyond. The Enlightened Masters don't believe in coincidence (s). They have told us that everything in our lives happened for a reason. There are reasons we fully understand as the consequences of our deeds, acts and decisions. And there are reasons we don't understand. Are they caused by others? Are they dictated by fate? Can we change the results, outcome and consequences of these reasons, and alter their effect on our lives, success, happiness, and failure? Yes, we can to a certain degree. This book will show you how!

The book includes:
* Factors which influence your future and luck
* The influence of the Anunnaki's programming of our brain and fate: A rare lecture on luck
* How to read Shashat; the screen of the unknown
* Rizmanah; Discover the calendar of your bad luck and good luck
* Learn how to remove your bad luck
* Learn how to create a good luck

* Daily chart/calendar of your good hours and bad hours in your life
* What to do and not to do during these hours and these days
* Best hours and best days, worst hours and worst days for
* Employees
* Booksellers
* Writers
* Investment
* Real estate business
* looking for a new apartment
* Buying gold
* Buying hard currency
* Selling your art
* Asking for raise and promotion
* Stocks and Shares (trade, selling or buying)
* For writing/submitting proposals and grants
* Job applications
* Meeting new people
* Selling new ideas
* Opening a new business
* Signing contracts, etc...
* Importance of your name in shaping good luck
* Writing/equating your name in Ana'kh Phoenician
* How to write/transpose your name in the Sahiriin language
* Map of United States lucky and unlucky zones
* Case Study: Unhealthy energy and vibrations that damage you and negatively affect your future
* Esoteric techniques you could use to positively influence or improve your future and business by protecting yourself against evildoers
* Grid useful for business, negotiations, meetings
* Foreseeing your future is not enough. You must protect yourself as well. Learn how to do it.
* Grid "Ain Ali" to be used to prevent others from hurting you
* Going back in time and creating a brighter future.

*** *** ***

How To Become An Effective Energy Healer And Master Of The Healing Touch

Handbook of Curriculum, Lessons, Training, Supernatural Techniques and Powers

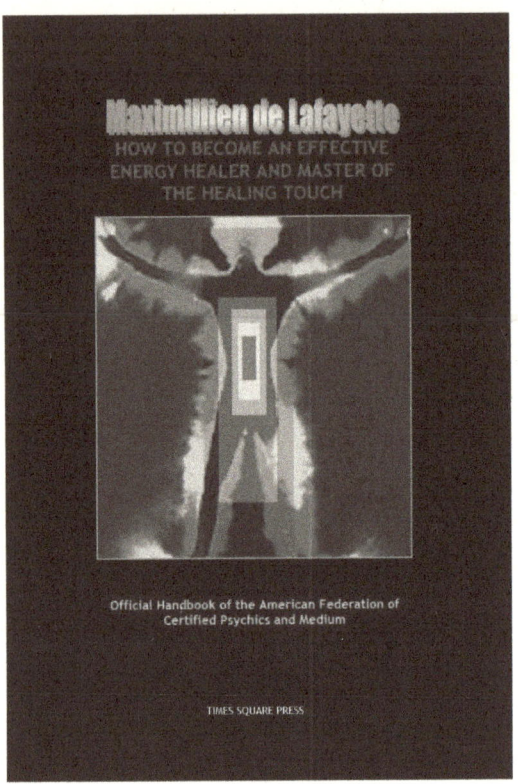

This book will show you and teach you how to become an effective and accomplished energy healer, and provide you with lessons, practical training, and step-by-step instructions on how to use the Healing Touch, find, learn, develop esoteric Energy Healing techniques which produce astonishing supernatural and paranormal results; techniques and know-how which were shrouded in secrecy for thousands of years; they are herewith introduced to the readers and the lightworkers as part of the curriculum and training/orientation programs of the American Federation of Certified Psychics and Mediums. The present work deals with energy healing and not faith healing, for faith healing belongs to strong religious beliefs, angels' interaction and a multitude of factors which don't fit in the scenario of scientific and metaphysical healing, and don't relate to the contents of this book. Thus, the study, exploration, training, and techniques as presented in this book pertain exclusively to bio-organic, mental-physical, and the extra-dimensional energy, emanated from the human body and the human mind, which can be revealed and detected in the laboratory, as well as in the immediate physical effects on the physical body, and our environment.

To become an effective energy healer, the practitioner must fully understand:
• 1-The nature of energy. In other words, what is energy? And how it works?
• 2-Sources and levels of energy.
• 3-How does energy (Bad or good) affect the mind and the body?
• 4-Techniques for animating and activating the practitioner's energy.
• 5-How does energy appear to those who can see it?
• 6-The meaning of colors of energy.
• 6- How to block negative vibes.
• 7- How to stop attracting negative people to your life.
• 8- How to discover the energy of the mind and the body
• 9- How to find energy's good days and bad days, and
• energy's good hours and the bad hours.
• 10- Ousoul; the universe's rules and the rhythm of the Micro Wheel and Macro Wheel.
• 11-How to reverse the flux of bad energy, bad days, and bad hours.
• 12- Mintaka Difaya: Protecting your zone.
• 13- The healing touch technique and mechanism, including the prerequisites and preparation.

The present work answers all those questions, and provides pragmatic techniques which enable the lightworker and practitioner to become an effective energy healer and master of the healing touch.

*** *** ***

THE ESSENTIAL MAXIMILLIEN DE LAFAYETTE: The Official Anunnaki Ulema Textbook for the Teacher and the Student. In 2 Volumes

THE ESSENTIAL MAXIMILLIEN DE LAFAYETTE is a synopsis of the 200 books, the author wrote on the subjects of the Anunnaki, the afterlife, the supernatural powers of the Anunnaki Ulema, the paranormal, the occult, parallel dimensions, multiple universes, the Conduit, the Supersymetric Mind, the Double, the Astral Body, communications with spirits and entities from the world beyond, the power of the mind, mediumship, channeling, the enlightenment, the Fourth Dimension, the Fifth Dimension,

Earth energy, healing, the world outside time and space, extraterrestrials, time-travel, reading the future, and similar topics. This is NOT a repetitious book. It was intentionally compiled from the most important concepts, theories, esoteric techniques, wisdom, Eastern philosophy, the world of the mystic seers "The Ulema", and particularly the teaching of Maximillien de Lafayette.

This series consists of 2 massive volumes, each exceeding 700 pages (50 MB). This manual is also the Official Anunnaki Ulema Textbook for the Teacher and the Student. De Lafayette wrote more than 800 books, 200 of them are in these fields. Consequently, it is quasi-impossible for the reader to purchase all these books. The present work contains knowledge, techniques and revelations, no other author has ever discussed, simply because they emerge from the teachings of the author's Enlightened Masters and his own philosophy. Add to the fact, that no other author or researcher has ever approached these topics, simply because they were brought to the West, for the first time in history, from the author's own vision and perspective. You will NOT find the material of this book in any other work, and/or in any library. As a matter of fact, the material of the present work (Volumes 1 and 2) is to a certain degree in sharp contrast with what it has been said or written in these fields. No one can claim that this book was inspired by or based upon any existing published book. It is a journey to new dimensions, and analysis of the physical and mental worlds as interpreted personally by the author.

The contents include: 1. Description of the Afterlife in all its states and dimensions. 2. What do we see when we enter the afterlife zone? 3. The various states of metamorphosis of the mind-body of a deceased person in the after-life. 4. Experiences dead people encounter in the next dimension. 5. How to bring good luck to your endeavors and surmount obstacles and hardship that prevent you from succeeding in life. 6. How to use Earth energy to your advantage and block others' bad vibes and vicious intentions that are causing you harm and damage. 7. The first stage of the afterlife during the 40 day period following death, and how to communicate with your departed loved ones and pets. 8. How the Anunnaki created us genetically 65,000 years ago. 9. The

mysterious and hidden world of the Anunnaki Ulema as the author knew it and explored it. 10. Foreseeing the future and rewinding time; revisiting your childhood and past life in different dimensions. 11. How the Masters, the Mounawiriin, and the Anunnaki Ulema transpose you from the present to the future? 12. How to develop The Supersymetric Mind. 13. Study of the influence of the Anunnaki's programming of our brain and fate. 14. The duplicate image of ourselves or reproduction of our body in other dimensions. 15.
The early human species and races created by the extraterrestrials. 16. How to learn The Anunnaki Ulema supernatural and mind power techniques. 17. Entering a parallel dimension; Is it possible to enter a parallel dimension and leave there all your troubles? YES!
18. Occult techniques and talismans to protect yourself from others. And much much more.-By Dina Vittantonio, Editor.

*** *** ***

Vol.2. Illustrated History of the Art, Monuments, Archaeological Sites, Cities, Gods and Goddesses of Phoenicia and Ugarit (Ancient history and Art of the Middle East)

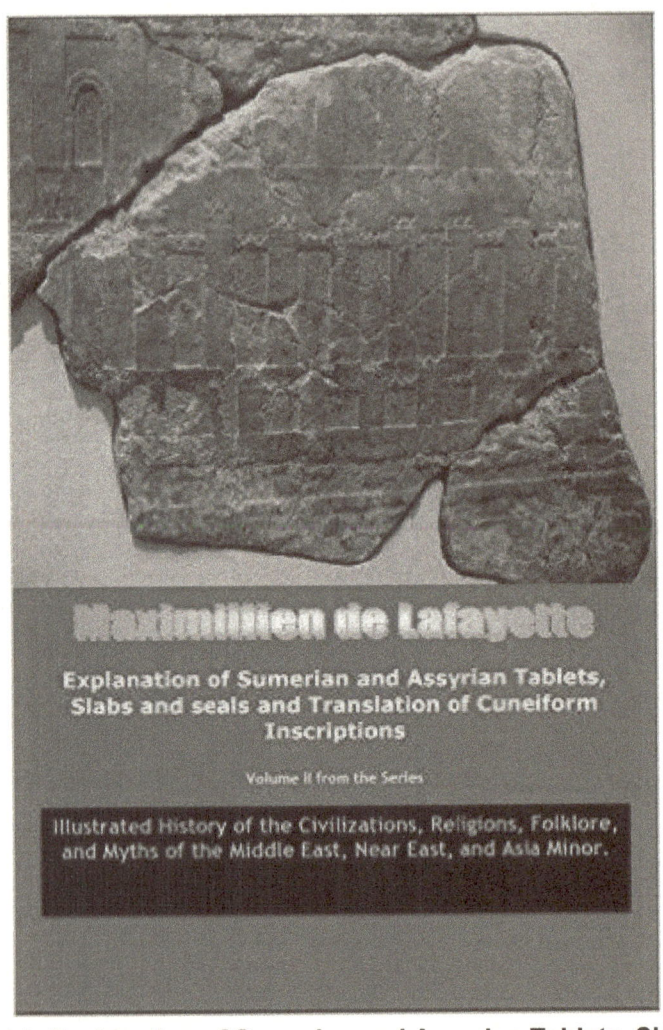

Vol.2. Explanation of Sumerian and Assyrian Tablets, Slabs and seals and Translation of Cuneiform Inscriptions. (Illustrated History of the Civilizations, and Culture of Middle East, Near East, and Asia Minor.)

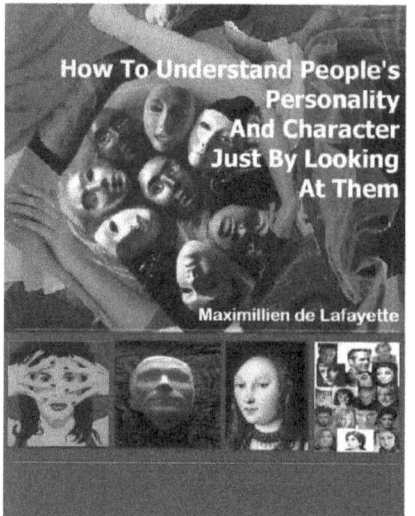 

From left to right: 1-How To Understand People's Personality And Character Just By Looking At Them. 2-The International Book of World Etiquette, Protocol and Refined Manners.

From left to right: 1-How To Understand International Law. 2-Comparative Study Of Penal Codes As Applied In France And Great Britain.

*** *** ***

Published by
TIMES SQUARE PRESS
www.timessquarepress.com
New York, Berlin

***   ***   ***

Printed in February 2023
by Rotomail Italia S.p.A., Vignate (MI) - Italy